24 Hou

THIS B

# Discovering Places of Worship

Izzi Howell

raintree

a Capstone company — publishers for children

Raintree is an imprint of Capstone Global Library Limited, a company incorporated in England and Wales having its registered office at 264 Banbury Road, Oxford, OX2 7DY – Registered company number: 6695582

www.raintree.co.uk
myorders@raintree.co.uk



Produced for Raintree by
White-Thomson Publishing
Edited by Izzi Howell
Designed by Rocket Design and Cl...
Picture research by Izzi Howell
Production by Kathy McColley
Originated by Capstone Global Lib...
Printed and bound in China

ISBN 978 1 4747 5394 4
21 20 19 18 17
10 9 8 7 6 5 4 3 2 1

**British Library Cataloguing in Publication Data**
A full catalogue record for this book is available from the British Library.

**Acknowledgements**
We would like to thank the following for permission to reproduce photographs:

Alamy: Hans Blossey, 6, Simon Balson, 14; Dreamstime: Brownm39, 30 (bottom), Draghicich, 8, Enriquecalvoal, 25, Jamie Frattarelli, 20, Masar1920, 24, Tupungato, 15 (bottom); Getty: Alain Le Bot, 16, Amanda Lewis, 10, esp_imaging, 4 (top left), FatCamera, 5, Feargus Cooney, 28, Gabi51, 30 (centre), Godong, 21, Gwengoat, 18, Huw Jones, 23, nadger, cover (top centre right), patty_c, 9, peterhowell, 22, ripmp4, 30 (top), stevenallan, 17, Ultima_Gaina, 4 (top right), umutkacar, 12; Shutterstock: Belozorova Elena, 27 (bottom), elvirchik abdrahmanova, 13, Christian Mueller, 7, Ilona Ignatova, 11, I Wei Huang, cover (bottom background), kaprik, 15 (top), kunanon, 29, Lizavetta, 19, Paul J Martin, 4 (bottom left), paul prescott, cover (top right), pingkung753, 1, 26, Sabrina Marchi, 27 (top), Shunsho, cover (bottom foreground), SmileStudio, cover (top centre left), Tom Gowanlock, 4 (bottom right), ...ft).
...ddhapadipa Temple in London.

Every effort has been made to contact copyright holders ...n this book. Any omissions will ...t printings if notice is given to the publisher.

We would like to thank ... Dr Suzanne Owen, senior lecturer ...s Studies at Leeds Trinity University, for her help in the preparation of this book.

...s (URLs) given in this book were valid at the time of going to press. However, due to the dynamic nature of the internet, some addresses may have changed, or sites may have changed or ceased to exist since publication. While the author and publisher regret any inconvenience this may cause readers, no responsibility for any such changes can be accepted by either the author or the publisher.

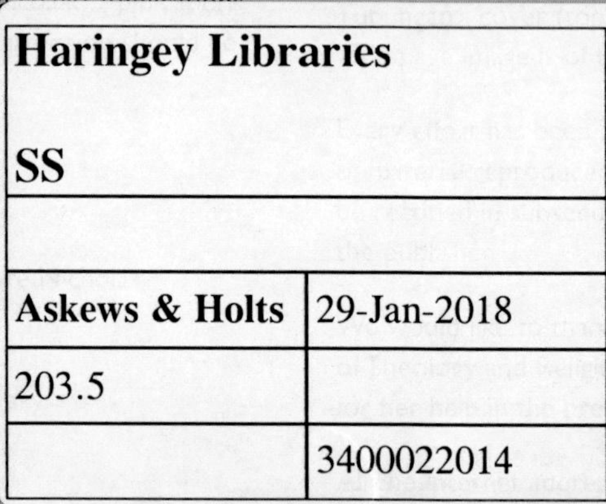

# Contents



Some words are shown in bold, **like this**. You can find out what they mean by looking in the glossary.

# Introducing places of worship

The six largest religions are Christianity, Islam, Judaism, Hinduism, Sikhism and Buddhism. People from these different religions **worship** in special buildings.

You might see different places of worship in your town.

People meet and celebrate in places of worship. They listen to religious leaders and share ideas.

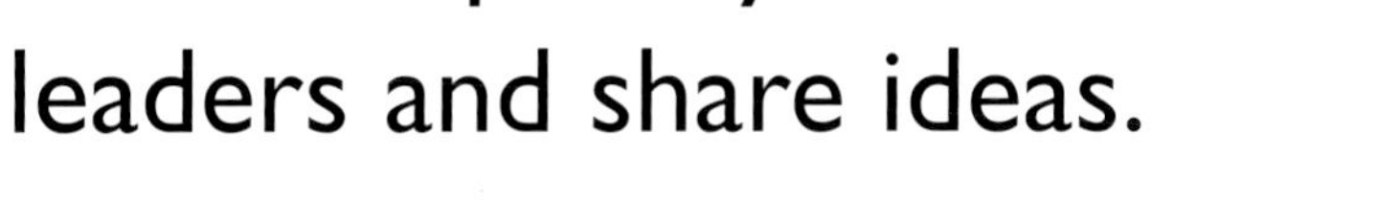

These Christians are singing songs together in a church.

# Churches

Churches are Christian places of **worship**. Some Christians go to church every Sunday. Others only visit on special religious days, such as Easter Day.

Some churches are cross-shaped. The cross is a Christian **symbol**.

Churches can be small and plain or large and decorated. Cathedrals are large churches. Some churches and cathedrals were built hundreds of years ago.

Christians often build tall churches to **honour** God.

At the front of some churches, there is an **altar** with a Bible and a cross. The Bible is the Christian **holy** book.

The **priest** decorates the altar with flowers and candles.

Many churches have stained glass windows. The windows often show stories from the Bible.

In this church, the priest stands at the front of the church to lead the **service**. The people sit on rows of seats to listen.

# Mosques

Muslims **worship** in mosques. Some Muslims pray at the mosque five times a day. Muslims also go to the mosque to study and to celebrate festivals.

There is a **crescent** on this mosque. The crescent is a **symbol** of Islam.

Mosques often have a **minaret** tower. In some places, a crier calls from the minaret to tell Muslims to pray.

Many mosques have curved **domes** on top. This mosque is in Dubai.

Muslims pray on the floor on mats. They face an **arch** called the mihrab. The mihrab marks the direction of Mecca, the most **holy** Muslim city.

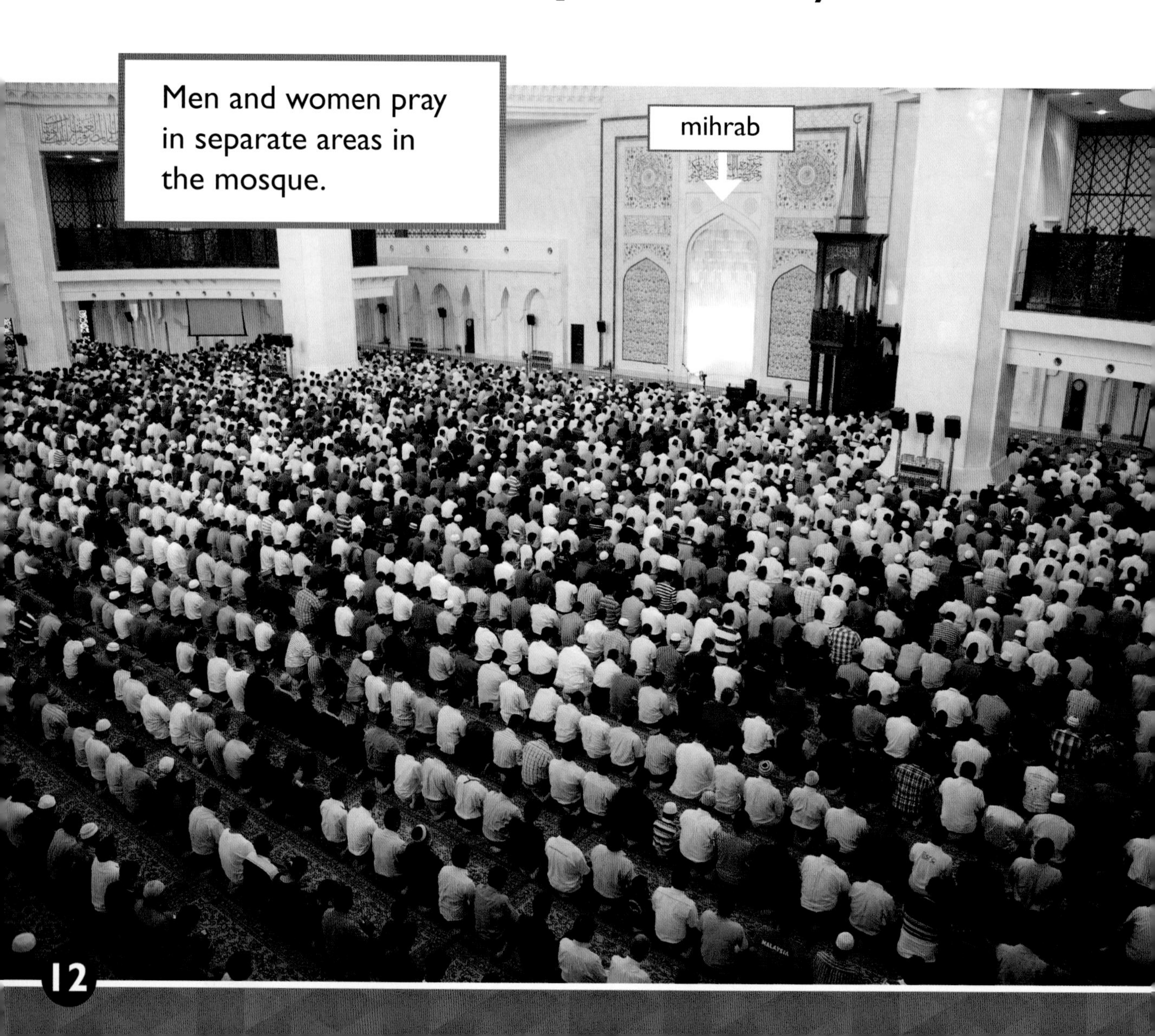


Men and women pray in separate areas in the mosque.

There are no pictures or statues in mosques. Mosques are decorated with words from the Qur'an. The Qur'an is the Muslim holy book.

Muslims rest the Qur'an on a stand.

# Synagogues

Synagogues are Jewish places of **worship**. The most important day for visiting the synagogue is Saturday. This day is called the Sabbath.

Some synagogues are decorated with writing in Hebrew, a Jewish language.

You can see different Jewish **symbols** on a synagogue. One symbol is the six-pointed star, called the Star of David.

Another Jewish symbol is the menorah candlestick.

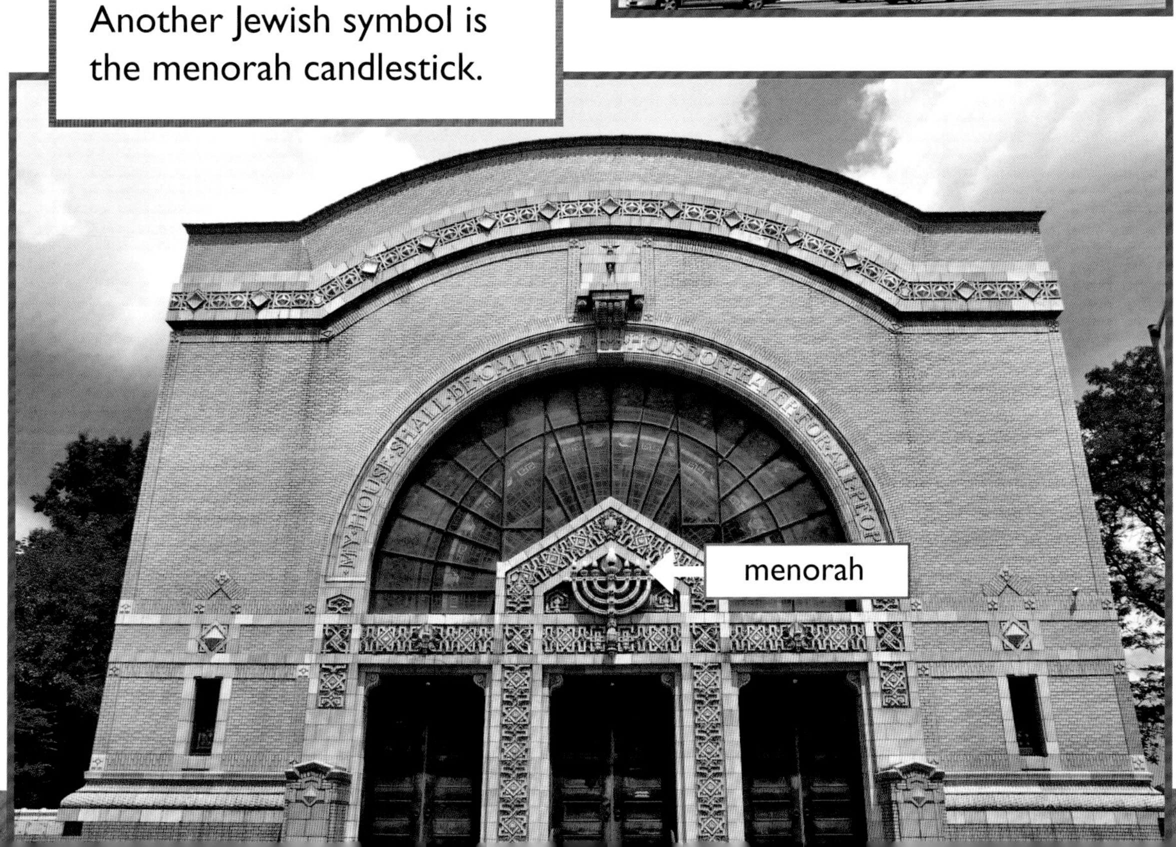

Jewish people sit to listen to the **service**. They face a special cupboard called the Holy Ark. Inside, there are **scrolls** of the **Torah**. The Torah is the Jewish **holy** book.

In some synagogues, men and women sit separately.

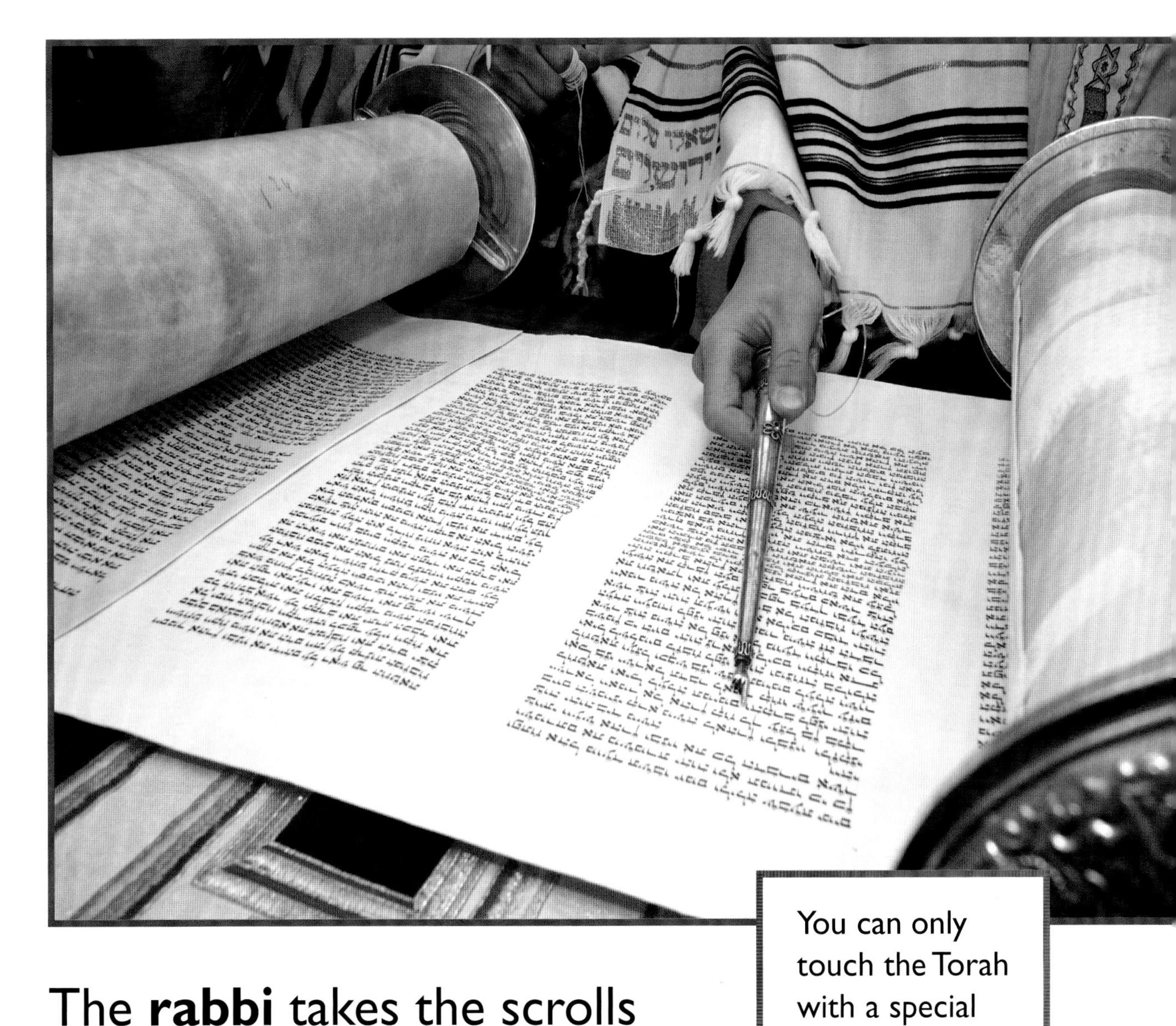

You can only touch the Torah with a special metal pointer.

The **rabbi** takes the scrolls out of the Holy Ark during the service. Then he reads from them.

# Mandirs

Hindus **worship** at mandirs. Hindu worship is called puja. Hindus perform puja whenever they can. They also worship at home.

Some mandirs have tall towers.

Many mandirs are made from stone. In some countries, the walls are decorated with patterns and characters from Hindu stories.

This mandir in India is decorated with **carved** Hindu gods and goddesses.

In the mandir, Hindus take off their shoes and ring a bell before they worship. They ring the bell to show the gods they have arrived. There are colourful pictures and statues of Hindu gods and goddesses inside.

Hindus pray in front of the statues.

The statues are decorated with flowers.

Hindus bring food and flowers to the mandir. The **priest** offers the gifts to the statues in a ceremony. Afterwards, everyone shares the food.

# Gurdwaras

A gurdwara is where Sikhs go to **worship**. They usually go once a week. They celebrate religious festivals at the gurdwara.

There are always four doors into a gurdwara. The doors are a **symbol** that people from across the world are welcome.

The Sikh symbol is called a khanda.

There is a Sikh flag outside every gurdwara. The flag is orange with a Sikh symbol on it.

Sikhs kneel on the floor to worship. They listen to a person called a Granthi read from the Guru Granth Sahib, their **holy** book.

The Guru Granth Sahib is on a **platform** under special cloths.

There is a kitchen and a dining room in the gurdwara. Sikhs cook and eat a vegetarian meal together after the **service**.

Sikhs eat together to show that everyone is **equal**.

# Viharas

Buddhists go to a vihara to **meditate**. They sit quietly and think. Buddhists do not **worship** a god.

Viharas often have a pointed roof.

There are often statues of the **Buddha** outside the vihara. The Buddha wrote the **holy** books of Buddhism.

Sometimes, parts of the vihara are decorated with gold.

Some viharas have an eight-spoked wheel decoration. This wheel is a **symbol** of Buddhism.

There are also statues of the Buddha inside the vihara. Buddhists kneel in front of the statues and meditate.

Buddhists place flowers and candles in front of the Buddha.

Buddhist **monks** live at the vihara. They study Buddhism and help people to worship. Sometimes, Buddhist monks **chant** lines from holy Buddhist books. Buddhists say the words with them.

Some Buddhist monks wear bright orange robes.

# Picture quiz

How much do you remember?
Find the answers on page 32.

1 Who worships here?

a) Jewish people
b) Christians
c) Sikhs

2 Where would you see this altar?

a) Gurdwara
b) Church
c) Synagogue

3 Which place of worship is shown here?

a) Church
b) Mosque
c) Vihara

# Glossary

**altar** table used in religious ceremonies, often in a church

**arch** curved shape over an opening

**Buddha** person who started the Buddhist religion

**carved** cut from stone or wood

**chant** to sing or say words in a special way

**crescent** curved shape that is wide in the centre and narrow at the tips

**dome** curved, round roof

**equal** same

**holy** important to a religion

**honour** to show respect for someone

**meditate** to sit in silence and think calm thoughts

**minaret** tower on a mosque

**monk** religious man who spends his whole life studying religion

**platform** raised area

**priest** religious leader

**rabbi** Jewish religious leader

**scroll** long roll of paper with writing on it

**service** religious ceremony

**symbol** picture that represents a religion

**worship** to pray or take part in a religious ceremony

# Find out more

**Books**

*Religions Around the World* series, Anita Ganeri (Raintree, 2018)

*Following a Faith* series, Cath Senker (Franklin Watts, 2018)

*My Religion and Me* series, Philip Blake (Franklin Watts, 2015)

**Websites**

**www.bbc.co.uk/schools/religion/**

Find out more about the religions mentioned in this book.

**www.bbc.co.uk/guides/z297hv4**

Explore the different parts of a mosque.

# Index



**Answers:** 1) a; 2) b; 3) c